The Other City

for my father

The Other City

Rhiannon Hooson

Seren is the book imprint of
Poetry Wales Press Ltd.
57 Nolton Street, Bridgend, Wales, CF31 3AE
www.serenbooks.com
facebook.com/SerenBooks
twitter@SerenBooks

ISBN: 978-1-78172-299-2
ebook: 978-1-78172-309-8
Kindle: 978-1-78172-308-1

A CIP record for this title is available from the British Library.

The publisher acknowledges the financial assistance of the Welsh Books Council.

Cover Image: 'Open the Door' by Michal Karcz

Printed by Airdrie Print Services Ltd

Author Website: rhiannonhooson.blogspot.com

Contents

Elan

There was a day, well into winter,
when the reservoir froze and we threw rocks
onto the ice, and never went back to watch them sink
as the hills shrugged into their thaw.

We never thought where they would come to rest,
till now; never wondered whose land their shapes
would mark. And beneath, dusk-lit in water's well-tolled
quiet, those houses filled with the rot of wood.

The squat gothic of the chapel, the gates sagging half
open, the dim mouths of doorways, not gaping
but softly parted into shadow, dust sifting
through the slow dark and there,

the little setting moons of our rocks: sinking
slower than you might think, robbed
of weight by water and turning slow. It's this
I think of now, when the soft knocking of the rocks

has long-since fallen quiet. I wonder
how many men are buried beneath the dams.
What do I know of conquest but this? The slow rise
of water; the fat silence of a quenched thirst.

The Sin Eater

After my great-grandfather's death,
his wife brought in a sin eater. I like
to think it had been raining, that day,
that he was weighed down with water
as she watched his approach
from her heavy-curtained window.

He must have walked up from the town,
a good half-hour's journey. His step
was light on the path, inaudible
in the steady drive of rain.
She would have made him wait on the step,
his Sunday-suit stiff with moisture,

and his hair slipping down his forehead.
She had not bothered to stop the clocks,
and in the dark hall they ticked to her time, now.
His coat stained the floor beneath the hat stand,
and she pretended not to see, ushered him
to a straight-backed chair brought in from the kitchen.

She cooked the meal herself, served
on the second-best china. The casket beneath the plate
had an enviable shine, and I imagine him
eating until the plate was clean, in small,
deliberate mouthfuls balanced on a heavy fork.
I wonder what she cooked him,

whether he liked it. I am told he was a thin man,
like a bird, as if food eaten over a corpse
could never nourish him. Besides, she would not
have given him anything rich, nothing so juicy
as a steak, nothing meaty. My great-grandfather
would not have warranted it.

Wintering

At the first frost, when cold made sugar
bloom meager into the sloes, cows
steamed the valley, down from the hillsides.

Geese woke us in the night. Larches turned
like old men toward the wind and let go.
In the house, pipes burst, the clock
stopped ticking, water came down the chimney.

The elm at the turn in the track dropped
its last leaves, held black branches
up to the stars. In the kitchen,
my mother baked saffron into the bread –
round suns wintering on the table.

Bulls

Zeus has a propensity for slipping
his flesh into the shape of a bull; stretching
his tough hide over its hulking frame.

He's always at it: witness the whip
of Europa's hair as she rides him
over the receding waves, sitting daintily

side-saddle on his broad back
and wiping wind-tears from her red cheeks.
He did these things under the moon

of precedent, though – had Pasiphae not fallen
for the bull that grazed at Gortyn, Zeus
might have stuck with an eagle.

Even the women are at it: Io trod a hundred
islands as a heifer before Zeus flicked his wrist
and she grew breasts again. Best not to ask

the fate of Ariadne, nor that of poor Asterius,
her brother. And now I come to think of it
didn't I, as a child, first come to know

of men while watching the white bull
in the field behind the house? The snow
was still patchy on the ground and he,

wreathed in his own steam, had the look
of a god, even then.

Suppers

Fridays they ate mackerel doused in flour
and foaming butter; bread to help the bones
go down, cut diagonally; he liked it better
that way. Already the century was half-gone,

the kitchen silent. Each supper was their last
supper. Each mackerel was the last fish.
And the frying pan was tempered black
by then – nothing would stick.

Saturdays she'd cook a chicken, an old bird,
feet crossed nonchalantly in the pot,
all yellow scrag. She'd pull the wishbone with herself
and wish for weight, body a blank. The bones

were good for stock, but nothing else:
they splintered in the dog's mouth, but in the iron pot
with carrots for sweetness they'd surface,
spiraling, and on Sundays,

in the afternoon, she'd sit to skim the stock
until it boiled cloudily clear, thinking how sometimes,
at the beginning, they'd eaten nothing
but warm fruit, choking sweetness into themselves

with ripe berries, white slices of apple
that drew sour lines across their faces; bread
and cherries. And then she'd find herself
seated at the table, each fish their last fish,

each supper their last supper,
the dishes piled up between them,
the black skillet lying empty.

it would be like this

you never buried the dog in its basket with your old coat
there was no grey in your hair
your face relaxed into a smile each morning
you unstuck your palms from perfect mirrors of water
and peeled it from your face in a film
the lights never went out
the clocks sucked their ticking from quiet rooms
people ate laughter with the dark solvents of their mouths
stole touches from each other's skin
you remembered how to hold your brother
in the tight heat of the womb
people ate songs out of the air until the air was hollow
and words unknit themselves
drifted aimlessly into the thin sky
so many forgotten things were remembered
and things held onto for too long were let go
one by one you unmade decisions
like following white pebbles through the dusk-lit wood
the universe inhaled

Facts, 8th January

Today the almond trees began to blossom in the streets
on the edge of Jerusalem; today
the mango rains fell in Salavan, and the fruits
began to ripen. In Washington the air between trees
was hazy with woodsmoke, and each pine branch
was slicked down with ice
and in Helsinki, where the sky is the same lilac
as the dress of a woman eating out in Padua
the sun set as children were leaving the schools.

In Santa Clarita the fountains froze. For the first time
in eighteen years snow fell gently there. People pressed their fingertips
to the windows, let their breath whisper the view, touched their lips
so softly to the glass.

Back to the North Field

Once I spent the summer's storms here, running
under the raucous geese along the cedar-lined drive,
long-since gated and blurred with grass,
empty hives lined along the fence.
We found three moles once hanging there,
dried to husks that rattled in the wind.

In the old photo we're stacked
up the limbs of the largest, my dangling laces,
my father looking so intently down the valley,
my grandmother against the trunk, eyes
shaded. Maybe the tree brought flashes
of memory for her: maybe the smell of hot dust
or the sound of a sprinkler running on the lawn;
maybe the stately spreading of another tree.

Remember this:
the book of stories she gave me, left out
in the rain, the pages stilling, relaxing
into the broken surface of the old driveway.

From Mongolia

I waited a year to ask for my suitcase back. I thought of it
in the corner of your room filled with those last favourite clothes,
those four best books, the one coat I judged
warmest, the boots which would last through a winter.
I pictured you packing it ready to send, the last
of my belongings creased and stuffed in so tight
that the case would burst at a harsh word. I remembered your shirts,
how you pushed them so carelessly into drawers, how creases
clung to them. I was afraid of opening the suitcase,
seeing how you had shoved the last of me away in a tangle,
crammed in more and more until there was nothing left,
and you could send it away, just away. I waited
until I thought I could bear the spill of tangled clothes.

But when I opened the case the clothes
were neatly folded, laid in careful stacks
which smelled of dust and milk.

Narcissus

Once, as we walked home in darkness,
you stopped and pointed down. Beneath
our hands' open-palmed clasp, the stars
were schooled like fish in a wind-flickered puddle.

That's where we live, you and I;
that world of reflections, the curved
infinity between two mirrors. Sometimes
I dream of you with eyes of polished silver;
it's dark, but a candle casts oily light.

And sometimes I'm afraid of being found
staring, blank and empty, into your eyes,
where my reflection blinks
and smiles a small smile
and slowly turns away.

Lady with an Ermine

The creature, cradled
against the yield of her breast,
smug foundling, lithe
as water, muscular as some furred
and unexpected dragon, its splayed toes
against velvet, that intimate touch
of ebony beads against its side,
but isn't it too just bones and heat?
Doesn't it plunge headlong
into the yawn of its final season?

She is calm as cool milk, hidden,
folded into herself again and again
like a wreath of origami, and after all,
it takes only one light touch
of those fingers
to hold the creature
still.

Brodick

How the sky curved hot above us,
cradled us as if within a sky-lined egg.
How the sand was cut with stones, pricked
with the paw prints of an absent dog. How we
licked the wine-soaked brine of mussels
from our fingers. How the sun dipped
but never set and seemed to hover delicately.
These things made us complicit in that place.

Above the mountain, eagles fell away
into the sky with such distant silence, skimming
their shadows over sun-smacked rocks
as we skimmed stones across the still skin
of the ocean. On that day everything mattered,
even the flickered jumps of sand fleas
at our feet, even the dead gull at the watermark,
and how it became beautiful.

Tracking

I smelt it, once, my mother's scent –
not the scent of her enveloping self
which meant, to me, a lit stove
and cheese to crumble into stew –

but the scent of her own childhood
announcing itself silently one summer
as the dust rose from the track:
Some bright-remembered place

where sun-dark skin flickered a shadow
through the lush stalks of sugar cane;
where the fan sliced through tepid air
above the veranda, and she,

avoiding the sour vermouth and olive smell
of her own mother, crouched on her haunches
in the dust behind the garage,
where the pistachio lushness of the car gleamed,

and Hazel's mahogany hands
wrung the thin neck of a chicken
or added beans to the can of stew
which hung above the fire.

Luminosity

A visit to Blackwardine led me to note on the map a straight line starting from Croft Ambury ... and through the high ground at Stretton Grandison, where I surmise a Roman station. I followed up the clue of sighting from hill top, unhampered by other theories, found it yielding astounding results in all districts, the straight lines to my amazement passing over and over again through the same class of objects.
From Early British Trackways Alfred Watkins 1922

Light always travels in a straight line
until you coax it elsewhere, and then
it flows like water, dripping from sills
and organising shadows into watersheds.

Other days it's frozen into rods, straight
as string for measuring. Nothing could stop it
then, only tinge it temporarily until the flood
of it crashed coloured through a window.

And there was a day, late June, walking
the marches when light resolved itself for you,
beamed across the landscape with sudden ferocity
so that everything became meaningful: barrows

stood proud of their sunken roots, the tall stones
announced themselves across the hills and you
were struck straight through with the simple, complex
web of it. Only later did you think of Hermes,

that subtle god of between-places, and of men
lighting beacons on the mountain-tops each spring,
fires burning in a chain, horizon to horizon,
thrusting up light to the stars like an echo.

And only then walked the old straight track back
to Blackwardine, seeing in each stride another mile
breached by nameless men, a flare of sight, as if
you were seeing all the land in the world at once.

Dough

failed chemistry
of sugar and yeast
leaves bowls of dough
unrisen beneath
limp cloth

my father –
who takes comfort
from the softness of dough
against his knuckles
knows the concave benevolence
of the bread bowl – tells me
his grandmother left dough
to rise by the fireplace
the black range open-roared
to the kitchen
her red fingers
turning the bowl
to make an even rise

how under the tea-towel
yeast hungered into air
stretched the fleshy
substance until it
rounded out
smug with purpose
like the white breast
of a dancing crane

I pull out arched necks
of dough
remember folding sugar
paper to make strings
of sharp-creased cranes
which scattered to the floor
in winter drafts

Years later men came to the house and catalogued the things they found. They sorted its dry discrepancies, the rooms filed like yellowing paper, the stacks of hatboxes, the glass bottles that were dull with cataracts of dust, the tinned food in the larder ranked and mellowing. They hid their faces with masks and damped down dust with sprays of water as they chipped off lead paint, uncovered doorways long painted shut and rooms resounding still with old silence. The house was written into itself, whispered across the stained and faded walls, scratched into the leaded window panes, marked out in the scattered leaves that had blown into the dining room. In the nursery at the top of the house they avoided the uneasy gaze of the old porcelain dolls, the bare bedstead creaking its springs. These were the last men to see anything of the house. Later still when the silk corsages and the blown eggs and the crystal decanters and the silver snuff boxes were packed in numbered boxes, and the house was left empty as a silent bell, they walked through the rooms of the house and left the subtle sadness that crept over them unvoiced. By then Virginia creeper had grown over the windows in the upstairs bedrooms, and the shadows there had the constant movement of light through water that rendered anything that entered in shades of blue and green. Patterns of light cast onto the floorboards shivered into life as the front door was shut. On the street the men watched the house shrink back and the windows deaden and the echo hollow out to nothing and did not think where it went.

How Women Are Not The Same

Remember: you were small enough once to sit
in your grandmother's lap and stroke the dry
crests of her curls. They had the softness of animals;
of mice, of moths, the fur behind a cat's ear.
When she died it was a simple thing to see her hair
tangling the rich earth, strands of it matted out
and sprouting from the ground like pale and delicate grass.
And remember too your mother laying out newspaper
in the kitchen like altar cloths, placing a chair
beneath the light with such precision;
the smell of newspaper and your sister's shampoo.
She'd left a salon once in tears, and since then
only your mother could cut her hair. It would end up
caught along the hedge for the birds to line their nests.
There's an envelope in an upstairs drawer
with a lock of hair, your name and your sister's name,
the strands mixed blond and brown. You think of it
growing there unseen, of threads that slowly twine
around the faded silks of your mother's underwear,
tangling the whole drawer full with its soft mass
and spilling down behind the dresser,
under the floorboards. Weeks after your sister left home
her hair was in the carpets. By then
you were transfixed with the fine lick of hair
against another girl's temple; with her tender hands,
the eczema on her elbows, her white halter top
that you tied up afterwards. The bow was wrong
but she kept it that way, anyway. You remember her
the first time I drape the length of my hair
over both our heads to make a dark tent for kisses,
when my hair grips your fist back.
And you've woken, haven't you, with my hair
in your mouth or wrapped around your throat,
with the dull length of it wound around your limbs?
It fills the bed and spreads through the dim house,
knots itself with bindweed and ivy, finds the roots
of the rhododendrons under the weak lime moon.
Feel it resting softly now against your cheek,
across your eyelids.

Samhain

My mother would not have it in the house
the urn dug from the barrow on Cefn Mawr.
Wrapped in my father's mud-cracked corduroys,

it came home strapped in the passenger seat,
fresh from the dig. My father left it in the barn,
where the owls exhale winter in their sleep.

In the house, my mother scraped frost
from the windows, put out the fire with cold tea
only to light again. Here the second season starts:

the fizz of green kindling, the line of boots
in the porch, an extra place at the table:
knife, and fork, and plate, all put away clean.

And all that night I thought of the silt
in the pregnant curve of the urn,
wondered if, in its sealed off world,

there shone a tiny sun,
trickling white light onto the landscape of ash
that slept, mindless, in its glare.

Being Dead

1

The pages are very small. He writes:
I am awake. Suddenly,
it's autumn. Outside the window
a rook struts across the blank lawn.
People are speaking, their mouths
are open. He laughs.

2

Suddenly, it's autumn. He laughs at the rook's strut
over the blank lawn. *10.27. This time, finally,*
I'm awake. The woman touches his hand.
The pages are very small. Perhaps
he's the orphan of a distant shipwreck.

3

10.27. This time, finally, I'm awake.
I was fully conscious at 10:35 am,
and awake for the first time in many, many weeks.

4

The woman touches his hand.
Suddenly voices fill the gap of his own mouth
and he's laughing. It's autumn, and the birds
have come to fill the blank lawn.
In careful steps they find
their own footprints and follow paths
back to the trees.

5

2:10 pm: This time properly awake.
2:14 pm: this time finally awake.
2:35 pm: this time completely awake.

6

He doesn't remember her, but he knows her.
When she is (suddenly) no longer there,
he asks the lawn
the flat-eyed birds
the bed, the chair, the walls
when she is coming back.
Then leaves are on the trees, and he is awake, finally.
The woman touches his hand.

7

I am awake.
10.27. This time, finally, I'm awake.
I was fully conscious at 10:35 am,
and awake for the first time in many, many weeks.
2:10 pm: This time properly awake.
2:14 pm: this time finally awake.
2:35 pm: this time completely awake.
At 9:40 pm. I awoke for the first time, despite my previous claims.

Origami

I can see you teaching this
to an empty room, how you run the crease
between finger and thumbnail, turn the paper
this way and that. The mountain fold turns your smile
away, silver sketching the bones of your face,
a napkin draped over a dish of plums.

The valley fold is your cupped hands, silence
of your absent thoughts; a cradled arm of logs
that burn dustily, a dish of plums beneath the window
where snow falls and casts its quiet shadows,
and beyond: the dark fringe of the wood
bowing its head like a black horse.

There is this, and little more: the house, the blanked
out lawn, one streetlamp and the torn edge
of the wood. But the petal fold is a dream you had,
and remembered years later: the barking of a dog
on a summer night, a girl, and how your hand
might fit the nape of her neck.

I imagine the rabbit ear fold hears how cold
might get inside you, grow whitely where there is no space
to grow. It is a neat desk beneath a window,
and how, asleep, you smile sometimes and nod
and acquiesce. Over time, things become precise
and we reduce ourselves to this: a dish of winter plums,

snow falling through the dim light
of a single streetlamp, the waiting of the wood
and how it sees us. We work paper
so we do not have to cover it with words. Here:
a paper flower in a dish of water,
on a small desk beneath a window

where snow is always falling.

The Placing of Objects

She lays out the silver, scant and tarnished, has me
sit opposite to stroke the cloth over the urn's bell curve.
It's empty: she threw his last grit out with the cats
into the yard; taps her gold tooth and says, *rain*.
Over the front door there's forked elder

the hoop that held the smoothing iron. See her
crack hazelnuts on the doorstep with it, wrapped safe in the
tea towel and after that broken. She took down
her net curtains to string the stream's green water,
a pool of minnows, her swollen ankles, twin tails
of the mayflies and woodsmoke rising through the trees.

I've changed, she says. I polish, nod. *It's fine.*
Lay out the table: one knife one cup one spoon.
Her fingers and their odd angles, faded stitches ranked
like dominoes across the table, ready to unravel. The oyster
sheen she paints on still and the smell of melting cheese;
the gate swinging shut. The gate swinging,

dust baths of the martins and how she says, *rain*.
Two women can sit and polish till the silver wears thin,
she's taught me this and how I am a woman, and how women
replace one another – not like the easing together
of the seasons, but like the river wears stones:

through attrition. There's a small smile surfacing then,
the bitterness of tea, her imprecise hands
sliding the objects into place for the comfort of it.
Lay out the table: one knife one cup one spoon. She says,
Go home, child.

Back

I watch the cat track finches
across the thin crust of snow
trembled weight not piercing
to the mud and time slips backwards
spools back that slick of sight
the cat's stealth slinking traceless and cowed
from the laughing birds as winter
thaws itself into autumn
trips back the leaves to their nodding boughs
has us walking to each dawn's dozing
steps neatly placed to erase our tracks

let us take back our birthday presents
turn away from each other and back
like magnets confused at our poles let time
lead us into summer
your mother
her dress
its chintz against the freshening flowers where
spring is caught in the year's throat and already
leaves grow back into the trees
and it becomes white again under our feet
the birds shrivel wetly
crawl baldly back to shells
that slam shut over their dozing heads
and the second turns inside out
and our hearts judder backwards
all this to watch you wake at dusk
and walk towards me

This Is The Time

It will begin like this: the shadows of leaves
on a white wall. And there I am. I'm always there
and quiet: only an outstretched hand, one pointed finger,
white profile like a Dutch portrait. Does that

make it easier? But words are not easy. Words
are their own beginnings and endings, splitting
like cells and growing, as if the page was a smeared slide,
the microscope mis-focused. Now we have admitted this
we can look away:

over here plants are straining towards the light, sounding
their stop/motion creak, birds are migrating, foreign cities
go about their foreign business. The feel of a man's palm
against your skin for the first time, remember that? That's
in there too, implicated in the swell of words. You don't know

how they fit together, their many combinations, only
that they do. Will you trust that I have written them
that way? No, you look to where I'm pointing, instead.
This is the time I get to look at you. This is the time
I look out from where I'm sitting and watch

you looking away, into the distance, at something
unimaginably beautiful.

Last Men

Because they did not see the white moon in its descent.
Because they did not hear the heron call, and in
the night when soft things whispered feathered words
they turned their faces into muffled pillows. Because
they never said their own names. Because in winter
they wrapped up too well in the thin sun. Because
they were healthy. Because the lamps
were turned down low. Because they spoke
in vowels and used polished spoons and because
when faced with fire, they thought of crumpets.
Because they could list too many things,
and with too many words; because they were strung
with pearls and polished plastics and when they dreamed
they dreamed of swimming, or of flying.
Because there was no forgiving, only restitution.
Because they forgot how to sing, and left soft-hummed notes
spilling from their pockets like wine gums.
Because the sun was too close, and the stars
too far away. Because they crowded the hillsides
like cattle or winter geese; because they said only yes
to life. Because they recycled. Because they did not recycle enough.
Because they knew too well how to love, and loved everything,
until there were only smooth pebbles of things
and the soft moon falling.

Flood

I dammed the river with my childish wants,
its small stones and smiles like flitted dragonflies:
one whole day spent between the banks and I

was nowhere, cold pressing through my boots
as the gravel slipped, fingers aching black with earth.
Downstream, sagging wire bridged the banks,

dredged leaves into rafts of green and stopped the violets
I crafted boats for. Next day a lamb was strung there,
swollen with water and the weight of its own wool.

It rose and fell slow as summer, one eye grey to the sky.
I saw it that night swimming downstream amid a school
of violets, diving beneath strung wire hung with glittered leaves.

Gulf

In Memoriam Tove Jansson

Think of it this way: the island
circled her, drawn tight
like a leather belt, extra notches
banged into it with a hammer
and nail.

Space enough
for the larch's rough silhouette
held tight against the sky,
yellow-leaved potatoes growing spare
on mats of seaweed. And at night:

ink blocks out
all complications, grows
outward and makes its own forms –

sweet and terrible,
but there's enough
in the bones of it
for you to lean free
of the page

blouse buttoned into the soft skin
of your neck, sun-worried and dark
with salt.

The boat is pulled up
well above the waves;
upturned, whole as the sky
above the pebbles on the beach,
each blind curve a world.
But they are shrinking,

shrinking, revealing slow grain
to the sun
as you have done.

Think of it this way: the island
is a circle; raw grey wood
beneath flaking paint, the stink of salt
and oil in winter, when the sea pauses
and the stove is lit.

Surely you knew it then: eventually,
the circle would close
to a dot.

The Heart

We have reached the age when our mothers are ill.
I was afraid to slip my hand into hers, but recall instead
the palmistry of winter streets: the drifts banked blankly
against the walls of the empty stadium, glassy fists
of fallen ice on Kossuth Lajos; how, in quiet squares,
the ground is sour with drifting lights, their tang of yellow
like silk pegged out to rot across the snow.

Over the ice-choked river, through the huddled streets,
we do not talk of how they broke your mother's breastbone,
how they sewed the muscle of her heart, flesh
to flesh; of the tear in that slick-bunched muscle;
of it straining and tearing and of it falling back
into stuttered rhythm, restless. We pretend
that winter's raw syllables are all we know:

birds calling their carbon drab above the streets, half-tuned
radio noise which spills from passing taxis, and beneath:
the plucked string of the lamp. The girl in huddled shadows
beneath the bridge. Bread is blood-warm in the pockets of her skirts,
which spread like cards: red, and pink, and gold, and black.
The heart. Our clenched fists together, the paper-scudded streets,
the sick dark rise of the sirens.

The Other City

Sometimes men go missing: warm tarmac,
turn of the key, the smell of newly laid carpet too
much. There are calls to be made, hours
to be unfilled, letters written and discarded,
whispered in the quiet dry space
of a car as rain falls, the arc of the wipers
and their wordless hush. Perhaps the glass steams
and slowly obscures everything, until only
the smell of dry cleaning and last week's one
cigarette remains. Only the radio tuned
beneath the rain, the letters unwritten,
the sudden precipice of the road, the measured tick
of the indicator. Sometimes men go missing.
They do not come back.

Look for them in a drab city of brick
penned in by a summer's haze, streets sluiced
with beer, see them always with their faces turned,
see them throng the empty parade ground,
cobbles smeared with the shadows of upright statues.
See them tread a muddle of alleys leading nowhere
and in the spring see them circle the bleached
clean skull of a horse, its brow stuck with smashed glass
which casts insects of light across their eyes,
the bridges of their noses, their hard
skinned hands that move so gently.

Horseman in the Snow

From a print of an exiled rider with his servant, by Katsushika Hokusai

In Hida there is an infant spirit
which comes at night to lap the oil
from lamps. Pathways open
between pine trees like mouths.
The slow hooves of your horse
would strike up sparks back in the village.
I liked to watch it in the rain. In Hida

grasses freeze, stretch out to meet the wind,
and you tell me, while I walk beside the beast,
pressing my scant warmth against its own,
of a boy you knew once, who lost the way
of himself in a blizzard like this one,
and woke with a snow spirit gazing down at him.
How do you make a snow spirit love you? I ask.

The horse's hooves in the snow are almost silent.
He went out walking in the snow just as we are
you say, *to leave her straw sandals he'd made*
and to turn away before the snow hid them.

I spend the night at the window
with a bare white flame, my heart restless in my chest
but no spirits come. Only the cold moon stains
the wide panes of the window with light.

Post

Bottles on the scrubbed front step,
her opening the door and finding there
a brother she had not seen in decades;
her shaken signature, the way she smiled
so tightly and thanked him for the post;
the way he shut the gate carefully behind him,
silence stretching between them all the way
along the street, ragged as it dragged the paving,
tangled along each neighbour's path. How
she did not watch him make his way up the hill
to where the town frayed into moorland
and men walked the morning out of their dogs,
but saw it anyway in the spotless kitchen,
as if he too unravelled to nothing at the edge
of the moor, and was lost once more
among the damp grasses.

Last Diary

First page was empty. Only her quiet tread
on the lozenge tiles, the clock that chimed
silence into the room
like the clapper of a thunderous bell –
and I knew it all already.

It still smelt of the drawer and its fragments:
one moth's wing and the dust-grey scent of lavender
lifting dry and decorous against my skin.
Three crossed-out words
their want
their small gazes.

I remember the bottle of violet ink that dried to flakes
of shining chitin against glass. This
and the swallowed silences that stayed the house,
kept it ordered through winter and there

on the seventh page
her script begins to fail
slumped vowels betraying each other

the pauses between them

the blank pages that came after
so few words
and all of them so small

Y Bedd

In a rugged steep place, where the waves
beat against the shore at Caer Cenodir
and the gulls dive sleek into the sea, I waited.

But the weight of these stones guards little,
save names; these names, this bone
of land where we, unflinching, crouch

to cast our lot and bow to strangers.
On the plain, beneath the sod of Llan Morfael,
on Long Mountain and Pennant Twrch, at the fords

and at the waters' meeting places we are buried.
Graves, though many, are all we have. Turn your back
on that sallow sun. Your prodigal muse
has always spoken in tongues.

The Englynion y Bedd – the stanzas of the grave – from the Black Book of
Carmarthen, record the resting places of fallen Welsh warriors in over seventy
verses.

Waiting for Ganymede

I had wanted to wait for Ganymede;
wanted – suddenly, inexplicably – to watch
as it crept around Jupiter's flushed cheek.
The metal angle of the telescope

gleams against the sky.
I bend to peer into that other world,
where we have found and coveted moons
like errant motes of rock caught motionless

and silent. Midnight settles over the snow,
and we, each in the crook of the other's shadow,
wait, our hands curled like dim flowers
around porcelain and milk; breathing

like bulls into the cold air. Under mine
your lips open, hot lotus blooming
into blackness. The world we found
in the lens is forgotten.

We are washed up
on the moon's tide,
the greying dark;
waiting for Ganymede.

Tipping Point

There's cold in the bones of the year. Clouds catch
in the beeches, hush the night down heavy onto cornered sheep
and tableaued at their heart, three black lambs watching the rain
from the fringe of the wood. I remember the strength I felt
that day above the dam, when the wind came in hot and dry
and me, twelve, heroic with a lost lamb under each arm.
The way they struggled, how the rough stink of lanolin and blood
was on them still, though the bleached moor teetered
on the hinge of the year. Things

topple. Water rises in the dark earth. Buzzards
tether themselves to the dyke and fall into the storm, angling
and turning, crying out. Years since I've touched a lamb,
years since the heat of them and the shrilled heart racing,
the darkness of the barn and blare of hunger. Later,
when the floods came, there were trees strung ragged with fleece
and bones. Now the black lambs sleep at the edge of the wood,
rain scouring stones from their sockets till the earth is blind
and I wish only this: let the rain fall into my mouth; let me drink it all.
Let the waters not rise again.

Fatale

This is the skin I wanted.

I wanted to shed my silks. I wanted to be white
as a fire beneath ice, wild as the spinning sun and grounded

as granite, but I was better broken open:
a thing ruined with starlight and towering fast.

I was there when Pikinni sang her last song; there
in the desert where the sand melted to slag.

I flew with Enola. I was the long hunger stuck
in gravity's throat. Call me Gilda, call me

Lulu, call me Bikini Helen; show me smiling
and riding the big bomb down.

And I know it was a joke to you, a way
to play at owning me. But

a star fell upon the ocean
and it had my name.

Thirlmere

After we lit the last candle
the gales couldn't hold us any more.
Along the lane the walls had begun
to slump, water sluicing through them
green as grass, but we drove
through anyway and out into the valley.

The fields were polished flat.
Trees were hung with drooping ropes
of fleece that caught the breeze like kudzu.
Banks of shale sprawled
draining across the roads, and the sky
was open, dizzying and blue, tall into the air
above the crowns of our heads,

and the slate face of the lake
was the same as always. Lakes survive
any flood, lie oblique in their hollows,
streaked with the half-truths of glimpsed reflections.
The birds were only then beginning to sound.
All across the fields the fallen trees were burning.

Fictions

At night we'd tell each other stories:
In Egypt, we fed at the pomegranate's mouth
long notes of languor rose from the ground around us
falcons hovered at their tethers' farthest reach
and swam the air like fish.
Russia's long night stank of dust
and furs. Our fingertips
melted tiny clarities into the windows.
We remembered looking out at snow falling,
how the caesura panned to let owls rise
silent as soft wax before the night resumed.
Fictions are precise like this. Somehow in winter
we came to the truth of it: how there were stars
once, formed from the hot weight
of a black other. How they hung
still and dark and raging and unknowable.
Nothing woke into the hot blankness of their reign
but we remembered them, and slept
fitfully, petty fictions sifting to dust
on the unswept floor, tangles of hair blown
beneath the bed, and the vastness of the stars only
inches above us, seeding silence
into the hot room.

Women Growing Old

The dry hollows of the hourglass,
the silences of stuffed birds, of china dolls,
the horrifying stillness of the rocking horse.
The ticking of clocks,
and the way old perfumes dry
in their glass vials brought from Russia.
The way the mirror's silver falls away
to lose a face one moment at a time.
Little chinoiserie birds with eyes
like dull silver spoons
always looking the wrong way.
And the spilled rouge and threads of tobacco on the dresser,
and the window rattling,
and the garden with its dying-back lilies in pots,
the sound of doors shutting and fire sighing,
the smell of candlesmoke and lipstick,
the way that dice will settle on a hearthrug,
and the laying out of cards.
The way paper curls and yellows, the way
snow falls past curtained windows when it's dark,
and the animals begin their winter sleeping
beneath the bedded-down dirt.
The way songs are forgotten:
each note losing the anchor of its word
and drifting into silence.

High Tide

I'll wake on that shoreline at the last of it,
thinking of the house in the photograph,
the rough bleached wood, the sun flaring breathlessly.
We might have sheltered in it when the waves became
too loud. We'd sit against the front wall
with our feet among the straggly samphire,
the frayed calls of gulls between us
like piled stones while the wind smacked
their trashy bodies to the water. Maybe the light
would hit the soft glass you find sometimes at the shore.
I think of that and the way the sun sheds its skins so whitely
by the water. The house never lasts.
The walls cave inwards, slump onto the solitude
of locks, the solitude of lost books,
of the sea beneath its tight stormclouds.

We run all rubbed to nothing under the grassy sky
our legs scratched, your palms leaving prints of sweat
on the pebbles. A photograph is only light and acids.
Later we sit in the wet car and on the shore in a half-dug pit,
black limbs of driftwood shallow into their own ashes,
and I am certain they keep the shape of a lintel,
the sills of windows, the smooth-worn steps
where samphire shrugged up between the boards.

S.S.

Times like these, every mist
is grainy over the damp cobbles,
the red lips of the women
on posters smiling, or not smiling,
and their skin monumental
over good, fine bones,
and their hair pale yellow, as if
the sun was always on it.

Times like these, even the echo
of a hard-heeled shoe has the city
awake, sweating in its bed. My god,
you can almost hear them breathing,
trembling, and the women thudded
with fear, biting their unwaxed lips.
They are never like the women
on the posters. Times like these,

if I'm honest, the cold gets to me,
even under the greatcoat, and the hat
that leaves a red band around my brow,
and my uniform, how the black wool
itches. And my hands: I can't
get the smell of leather off them.
In a narrow house by the river, even the dog
noticed, wouldn't stop sniffing at them,

and the boy – all sickly skin and dark eyes –
they say that's what they all look like,
but how can I tell, when the whole
country is so cold? The boy just stood
by his mother's chair and never
made a sound. The whole place smelled
of their sour food like yeast and vinegar,
and on the stove dumplings boiled dry

and began to burn. After, I shot the dog
with my pistol in the alley and felt,
only then, any pity. But times like these,
when only the women on the posters smile,
everything seems the colour of a closed eye:
red, black; the glinting silver of those two initials
on my uniform that let me admit my pride.

Without Narcissus

The lack of his blindness shocks the silver water black.
Your palm's slap against its surface is looped silence:
bare shoulders with their heron stoop,
the wet ropes of your black hair, the empty water
and the stiff-leafed lilies which break for sharp fingers,
their pink throats silent and smiling. Speak.

Over the water the red rock leans and watches.
Your nails like fish-scales break against
the cool shadow of its noon, and the silence. Speak.
Even the fish have voices, even the rough
hush of the trees, even the birds. You press your body
to the dark-loomed sediment and learn its silence, touch the red
heat of your mouth to the rock and learn the syllables
of its unspeech. Speak.

Birds watch you writing the mangled sign of your name
wet hair strung across the tangled mats of cress,
white fingers and their fish-belly pallor, your white lips
kissed against the petals of the lilies. You can speak
their silence back to them so well, so well.

How To Become Yourself

Dream sometimes of your own reflection.
Wake pulling at your flesh or the flesh
of your lover. Stab straight through the meat
of the Sunday joint to watch the juices run clear and say
this is my self. Ignore the feeling of rising you sometimes get
in the bath and the feeling of falling when sleep paws at you. Ignore
the way your mind fires words at the end of the day, and how some of them have voices
of their own. Read the books your father recommends. Sleep. Cut down the sycamore by the back door and
burn the green wood, dodging sparks of hot sap and do not cry. Correct your mistakes or better still hide them,
hide the doors with newspaper and masking tape and lines of salt and ash, ignore the birds in the attic the birds
throwing themselves at your windows, sleep. Let your dreams wash off you each morning. Do not record them,
do not fill a book with their spreading narratives do not let them cloud your walls, your windows, do not write
messages on glass. Keep surfaces clean. Sleep in and get your rest.

(Keep stones from foreign countries in a box of dust
and one day spit into it to grow a seed.)

Penthesilea

Her hair lifted into colour
by the dawning blood; wounds so softly
visible across her skin, stroked there
like silence, like the spreading of ink.

He lifted her body, broken
amid the tall smoke, and kissed her mouth.
She was beautiful beyond despair;
heady blood dripped slowly

into the rich red earth,
and the river. I heard only hoarse breathing
scratched under the shrill cries
of falcons, and beyond that

nothing: mere ideas fallen to the dirt
like so many plumed helms.

Wake

Afterwards, I wiped the mirror clean.
In that marred silver we were all ghosts;
blemishes cast the shadows of themselves
onto my cheek, refusing to be hidden
even under the stroked tendernesses
of her maribou powder-puff. I sat with dust

on my palm while downstairs people
made each other remember; sat
with dust on my palm at the dressing table,
you a dark glanced shape on the bed behind me,
and I painted my fingernails, three strokes
to a nail, *rouge noir*, Chanel.

It smelt of pear drops. I took out my earrings,
laid them neat in a row and clipped the ache
of her pearl and gold clusters to my ears. One
had a stone loose, tapping as I turned my head,
like her long nails against the side of a glass
and you were quiet, suddenly, standing

to tuck my hair behind my ear
running your thumb down slow behind it.

The House on Fire

Paper burns the fastest. And the dried flowers
you leave on all the windowsills, and the piano
flaring its final silence. All that silver
running to mercury. The noise of it fills each room
until the roof angles up off its beams.
In the bathtub your hair splays out like white
weed. The wallflowers dozing against the porch
slump into their own scorched scent.
Each room breathless and slamming its doors,
flames leaning down to touch the water –
Then we're walking through the ruts of the frozen field again,
my red wellies, the dry sheets of ice that crack like toffee,
the horses echoing out the mist and nuzzling velvet
into the palms of our hands. And you're in the kitchen
cutting puffballs with the bread knife, and you're sowing
crumbs into the flowerbeds, and saying
not yet. Not quite yet.
Then you're striking matches at the cooker
with your swollen fingers all bent
and the phone is ringing,
and the light is in my eyes. I've seen ghosts
pour like water through a dim room, white things,
weak things that scatter in a draught, and now I see you,
and how your ghost is like fire: roaring,
laughing, eating.

Beacon Hill

Above the house the hills were ragged
with wind, with late summer
and all its dying grasses. We drove up there
for the sake of driving – I'd not been home
in so long, I'd forgotten the smell of it.
You'd seen a fox up here a month ago,
a big male. He'd run across the road
before your car, and you'd watched him
crossing the high pasture in the moonlight
down to where the dense pines begin
beyond the farm. I envied you that, god,
so much. I'd seen only one in the garden
since leaving, and I felt so foreign up there.
Every night the wood was empty.
But he'd run across the road and onto the warm
dark grass, the biggest you'd seen,
running with the sort of grace nature has
when it is not afraid. And when we reached the curve
where the road turns down towards the pines,
he was there. Hung over the fence, dead,
of course. Of course. I'd not been home
in so long, I'd forgotten it, all of it, the sound
of the wind up there on the tops, the taste
of the air, how things find a way to you,
somehow, if you wish for them too much.

Ullswater

Years later you'll wake drenched with the moon's
long downpour of light, the silt of it over everything.
Through the windows the frost-pastelled shadows
of hedges will be smudged all across the hills
like lines in chalk. You'll see them
leading off along tall horizons
and with your fingers walk the wavered glass
to where they scrub themselves out, falter
into tumbled walls which scab the matted bracken.

Wind along the watersheds is thick as water –
by then you'll know this, and know also the paths
that sheep take over the tops, how they follow
blind contours down towards the water.
You can drink the silence above that lake.
You'll remember it as you look out
over the moon-lifted landscape, remember
the weight of air and the greenish quiet drifted
beneath the surface. It isn't that water
has covered everything, though it's seemed that way
since your feet first found the cold edge of rock
leaning out over sudden depth;

more that the weight of it has got inside you,
and you remember how it feels to drown
since swimming there, how a fingertip pressed to your eyelid
will coax light from dark the way the water did.

In Spring

There are leaves like hands opening
and the old queen in her rotten palanquin
teetering along the road, stones
in the black ground opening like eyes
you open your mouth to sing
the road bursts into blossom
ticks fall from the backs of horses
nests from the eaves.
In attic rooms fanfared with creaking ropes
poets hanging quietly sift into insects,
find cracks, escape
and burrow into the bronze shock
of the sky. Those pinkly newborn children
uncurl on their pillows and speak new words
to their mothers, new soft words
from their soft palates
and soak up sun on all the windowsills
like fat hairless cats, watching.
What gods come, come stalking on all fours,
lean, and hungry, and afraid.

Within the City

the world tilted into wakefulness
sky humming the bleached note through him
even his bones

the throat of some slack shore slumped into city
forced out of its state
across streets jaded with souring light
dopplered in narrow hallways
green with moss-lit skylights
such riotous quiet stumbled
into him
he thought he saw it
and he reached out --

hair sprawled through the
croquet hoops

spool the glimmerdark bodies dense

the broken facade
of the mirror darting a

small bitter smile

Half-Self

Home left hard. I lay turning in my own dumb heat,
dragged by the last limp weight of home,
clutching my sickness to me. I fed my fever
through the night, morsels of smoke and dust,
pulled pain from my throat in long knotted strings,
but still it passed, left me trembling and bereft,
stumbling blind into the morning. Flesh fell from my bones,
dawn blasted the last of my first self free.
In white rooms where the slow dust settled
light unmade me, shook the walls, seared my skin,
turned my bones to embers of themselves,
and the sad stray dogs on street corners
began to howl for meat.

Yes, it left me deaf and dumb.
Yes, I crawled and grasped and retched,
yes mother I am lost, yes I am alone, yes I leapt from the edge
of the spinning world. Yes I quake
beneath the blaring dawn yes
I am a new bare lump of bone and blood and dust
speaking silence and unformed words
a thing astounded by itself and understanding nothing
a thing opening its eyes to the dust storm
a thing just beginning to grasp that what it hears
is a song.

Autumn

Some of it's easy: the dim room,
the sound of a mattock on a metal pole ringing
through the fleecy air, a voice whispering *oh oh,*
the geese who slap down winter from their wings
and huddle the leeward hill to stop their hunger
with the staunch grass between rocks. A leaf on the bedspread,
and that hush of trees loud enough to chase me from a dream.
Then there are the spiders waking into the rush of themselves,
not the dozing summer spiders like scraps of cut hair,
but the ones that run at you in fevered recognition,
disdaining walls for the open grassy spaces of the carpet.
The last of the flies are slowing down,
fat bluebottles with their iridescent backs
like sparks chipped from the rubbing together of our world with another,
to die their tiny deaths drowsy with the oven's heat.
This teetering at the tipping point of the year leaves
everything restless. Things know themselves for what they are not.
The lane scuds down to bedrock and finds water.
The wide lawn remembers a dream of women crawling
like dogs, their dark mouths swinging slack and spilling moss.

How It Finds Me

perhaps on white feet through snow
perhaps on the softness of needles
banked beneath pines
in drifts of blown wool across shattered slate
the slumped wet clothes behind the bottle bank
the boggy lawn with its rakish moss
the lane after the hedge cutters
their thrashing metal

perhaps forgotten in carrier bags with folded receipts
perhaps now
perhaps now

I'll wake to find the prints of small feet
shoved down into mud beneath all the windows
the ground will be dark with them
grass flattened all the way to the wood

perhaps on white feet
delicately avoiding snowdrops
through the last thaw

Owls

Sunday, and a barn owl flies into windows
silted with dusk, lies quiet on the earth
until the garden dims.

I spend an hour watching the body of the bird
and how it moves in sleep like the slow
swimming of a fish, the soft clockwork
of a body in motion.

Sounds can hollow a different darkness:
there was a game I had once, owls calling
in the wood, asking *who, who,*
and how I answered *here.*

Waking, the barn owl fades into movement
and is gone, but returns the next night
as if those hours of oblivion on the neat grass
of the lawn had offered some deeper darkness,
the deaf–dumb refuge of the egg.

The Gap

No, listen: a new door opened in the house.
During the night the walls slid apart to taste the sour edge
of new geometries, perspectives yawning and hungry
for light, scraps of paper which it sifted to dust
sliding in slow draughts like curtains of cloud above a high hill.

Remember when we could spend a day
reading patterns from a pack of cards tossed to the floor?
Or dropping books to the bed and finding destinies
in the open page? This dark door could not be played away
like that. And what else is a book but a narrowing of fate,

slivers chipped off like pieces of flint one word at a time
until the whole has honed itself to that final, inevitable, point?
And this other room: I spent days nursing the black
mouth of it, reading through those long afternoons,
throwing in words just as a bird feeds her young:

from her mouth to theirs, and some of them mispronounced,
and some of them foreign, and some of them unknowable,
each sound tumbling in: tiny, and singular, and lost
quickly in some unseen cathedral to absence. But
in their tumbled fall they scraped away so many atoms,

smoothed the dim walls slick, and came to rest like silt
or like the drifting pinpricks of algae which betray
the vastness of tides. No echoes made it out.
I played patience with the widening hole in the wall.
I set out the cards and turned each in turn, knowing

their felted corners, their creases and how the queen
might turn her back on kings to watch with biro-blinded eyes
the blank space at the edge of the carpet. I listened
to its silences. I sang to it. I raged and ran a metre in
only to turn back chilled, subdued, as if silence

was a disease to be caught; as if that secret space
was too massive to ever be filled. Think of it
like this: in the garden sycamore sap dripped
onto my mother's washing, worms beneath the turf
mistook my running footsteps for rain, and fled

the chambered safeties of the earth. Clouds slammed shut
above the fields where cows were watching one another.
I led my mother back inside to point into the smug darkness of the door.
My mother's hand pressed to her lips: think of it like that.
How many words stopped behind her hand?

What was the shape of them in her throat? Now think of sand
at a river's mouth. Think of each grain that comes
to settle in the soft bowl of gravity beneath the currents;
its dithered fall, the way it drifts like snow
on the curlewed moorlands, the way words are piling

one atop the next even now, the way they mouth
each others' sounds. Think of these things
and see a day of rain falling into the vast gap of air
above a canyon. See salt scattered
across a red lacquered floor. See me

reading at the mouth of a great dark pit. *The rabbit-hole*
went straight on like a tunnel for some way, and then dipped
suddenly down.

Leaving

There was no road for us, and the lake beds
with their smooth mud were like eyes closing.
Yes, we drained them one by one behind us,
and we tore up the hedges, and we kicked at the lime-
stone walls until they toppled. We walked on
with our pockets filled with words, little papery things
which we traded at night around the last fires
and shuffled, and remembered, and forgot.
Tea, we told each other. *Siren. Mother.*
By then the leaves were turning
and the trees were lifted from their drab.
We remembered them also and burnt them whole:
great torches flaring up against the deepening cloud.

The hills eventually turned to dust. Squat cottages
slumped into scree, and the tough sheep wintered
into fleece and bones, and we turned our back
on rain and honey, a hundred years of home.
When the fog fell onto us we raised our faces,
and walked on with empty pockets, hoping
to happen upon new vocabularies. But until then,
until the day when the fog lifts and we remember a new place,
how can I hold all this in the palm of my heart?

Daughters of the Dust

There can be no mermaids of the steppe
though its bare hills roll and boom like the sea. Only
some stranger creature, lithe in the gelid dust
and furred like a fox: silent, accusing in the eyes,
a deep wind parting fur down to bone coloured skin.
Horizons pile thin as paper one atop the next
and they spin their story into the pinched air: a woman,
and a wish, and a corsac fox. Nights

of the great white zud they might dance away the snow,
leaving paths of grass for the herd to eat, or else
rise like walls to blow across the landscape
stately and slow and sickening, only the chiming ice
singing their welcome with its spare high notes,
each like the prick of a needle. And in the city,
where the nights smell of sweet smoke and milk
and idling traffic, they go walking now:

silent over the glaze of blood frozen to the ground
around the wrestling palace. Silent in the alleys
where stray dogs sleep in the warmth from sewer grates.
Silent past the cafés where soldiers thaw their brows
over salt milk tea. Silent, until they are singing,
each alone in the dim reaches of the night,
each pale as an unlit candle, up through the gers
where the roads falter and the lights go out; up to the mountain
where the wind sings back; towering, and tidal, and old.

Acknowledgements

This collection would never have been possible without the support of Graham Mort and Lee Horsley, who supervised my PhD with enormous wisdom, insight and patience, even when I ran off to Mongolia in the middle of it. I am so grateful to both of them.

Several of the poems included in this collection have appeared elsewhere or been published previously.

'Y Bedd', 'Elan', 'Waiting For Ganymede', 'The Sin Eater', and 'Bulls' appeared in *Seren Selections*, edited by Amy Wack and published in 2006 by Seren.

The following poems were included in a short collection, also called *The Other City*, which was awarded the 2008 Eric Gregory Award: 'Origami', 'Elan', 'Wintering', 'Bulls', 'Suppers', 'Narcissus', 'Luminosity', 'Samhain', 'The Placing of Objects', 'How Women Are Not The Same', 'Gulf', 'The Heart', 'The Other City', 'Horseman in the Snow', 'Thirlmere', 'Women Growing Old', 'Without Narcissus', 'Penthsilea', 'SS', 'The House On Fire', 'Wake', and 'The Gap'.

'The Sin Eater' appeared in volume 39 issue 4 of *Poetry Wales*.

'How Women Are Not The Same' appeared in the Autumn 2008 edition of *Magma Poetry*.

'Fictions' was runner up in the poetry section of the 2009 Bridport Prize, and was published in the anthology of winning work.

'Daughters of the Dust' appeared in the anthology *Heavenly Bodies*, published by Beautiful Dragon Press is 2014.

'Fatale' appeared in the anthology *My Dear Watson, the Very Elements in Poetry* published by Beautiful Dragons Press in 2015.